Mo

Best wishes
from
Ms. Waghitha Parween.

Susan Philip

Prodigy

Mother Teresa

First Edition: April 2009

64 Pages, Price Rs. 25

Printed in India.

ISBN 978–81–8493–139–6

Pro–ya–en–40

Prodigy Books is an imprint of
New Horizon Media Pvt. Ltd.
No.33/15, Eldams Road
Alwarpet, Chennai – 600 018.
Phone : 044 – 42009601/03/04
Fax : 044 – 43009701

Email: support@nhm.in
Website: www.nhm.in

PRODN / 02 / 05-09

1

'Give until it hurts'

'Mamma, Mamma!'

The twins were back from school. Their mother hurried to open the door, and the girls burst in, both of them talking at once, as usual.

'Do you know where we're going next week?' asked Neetu. 'Guess where Miss Peters is taking us', shouted Neena.

'Girls, girls', said their mother, laughing. 'One at a time, please.'

'We're going to visit an orphanage Mamma', said Neena. 'Miss Peters said we were to bring something to give the children there', continued Neetu. 'She said we could bring whatever we liked, but to make sure it was something new and useful, which the children would enjoy.'

'What shall we give, Mamma?' asked Neena.

'Let's think about this, shall we', said their mother, laying the table for tea. 'We can ask Papa for ideas as well.'

'Why is the school taking you to visit the orphanage?' Mrs Patel asked a little later, watching her hungry 12-year-old girls while they ate.'

'Miss Peters takes Moral Science, and we are learning about being responsible for those less fortunate than us', said Neena. 'So she thought a visit to the orphanage would help us to understand the lives of children who are not lucky enough to have good homes like us', continued Neetu. 'She said it would also teach us about giving.'

'Ah yes, giving', said Mrs Patel. 'That reminds me about a wonderful person whom I met one day when I was a college girl.'

'Oh tell us about it, Mamma', said both the twins together. They loved hearing tales about when Mamma and Papa were young.'

'Hmmm...yes, I remember that day so clearly', began Mrs Patel. 'We were in the college auditorium. The hall was full of chatter. What else would you expect from several hundred teenaged girls with free time on their hands? We laughed and gossiped happily, discussing fashion and food and family and friends while we waited for a special guest.'

'This was in the 1980s, and the whole college had gathered to meet a very famous person. All of us present there that afternoon knew of her, of course, but I don't think anyone, including the lecturers, had actually met her in real life.'

'Who was it, Mamma?' asked Neetu, the impatient one.
'Wait, let Mamma tell it her own way', said her twin.'

'We had been waiting for a while', continued Mrs Patel. 'Like it happens so often when young people are gathered together, at some point a few girls started singing a chorus. Soon the whole auditorium was singing lustily, old favourites and the latest hits. Someone started *'She'll be coming down the mountain...'*, and we giggled as we sang *'she'll be wearing white pyjamas when she comes, when she comes'*, picturing our VIP visitor in those clothes. We found the idea of nun–yes children, that's what our expected guest was–wearing such clothes very funny indeed.'

'I think most of us in the hall that day thought of nuns as not quite human, imagining them to be forever serious and dignified, people very different from us, people who had never been young, never laughed and were boringly good.'

'Then, 'Shhhh.. Shhhh', said those who were waiting at the doors of the auditorium to welcome the guest. 'Quiet, girls! She's here!'

'We fell silent and craned our necks to see the woman we had been waiting for. Imagine our surprise when we saw a tiny little person zipping down the shallow steps that led from the outer doors to the dais, with the Principal and other authorities rushing to keep up with her.'

'Seated on the stage, she looked even smaller. She stooped and had a million wrinkles criss-crossing her face. She was dressed in the white saree with its ink-blue striped border which is the mark of her own special family of nuns, or 'order', as it is called in the Roman Catholic Church.'

'Can either of you guess who our guest was?'

'I know, I know', chorused Neena and Neetu. 'It was Mother Teresa, wasn't it?'

'Yes, it was Mother Teresa of the Missionaries of Charity, Nobel laureate and winner of so many other awards, the woman who shook hands with Presidents, Prime Ministers and Popes and with the same hands cared for the sick and the dying poor in the most ghastly conditions', said their Mrs Patel.

'I remember thinking … 'But she's so small and old.' I'm sure most of my college-mates were thinking the same thought that day.'

'When Mother Teresa got up to speak, however, we forgot her size and her wrinkles. We saw that she had sparkling eyes which darted about the hall. And she had a mischievous smile. She seemed to be talking to each of us personally.'

'She told us that day about giving. Not giving, as we had been doing for so many years – giving bags of old, unwanted clothes to the poor at festivals like Christmas, or after natural calamities like floods, giving a couple of coins to beggars on the roadside, even buying a few new things like soaps and toothpaste for distributing to needy people and feeling that we'd done our duty.'

'The giving she was talking about was different. She told us that true giving came out of love, and when we gave from love, we gave what we ourselves needed, putting others before self. *'Give until it hurts'* was her message that day. Give until it hurts, not only to friends and family, but to all those who are in need. It was another way of saying we needed to love each and every one of our fellow human beings.'

'It was an extraordinary message from an ordinary woman who did extraordinary things.'

'Where was Mother Teresa from, Mamma?' asked Neena. 'Was she a Bengali? I know she worked mostly in Kolkata.'

'Well, yes, and no', replied Mrs Patel. 'Her life began in a far-away place called Macedonia. She started her great work in Calcutta, as it was called then. But really, she belonged to the whole world.'

'Let us follow her through her life, from Macedonia to Calcutta and beyond…'

2

'I was expecting to be free, but God had his own plans.'

'How did Mother Teresa become a nun, Mamma?' asked Neetu. 'Was she always holy and good, even as a child?'

'A lot has been written about Mother Teresa and the things she did which made her famous', replied Mrs Patel. 'But very little is known about her life as a child. This was mainly because she herself was not very keen to talk about her early years, and wasn't really eager to share details about her personal life and feelings even later.'

'I remember trying to find out more about her after that meeting in the college. I put together bits and pieces of information collected from various sources.'

'We do know for sure that she was born in the year 1910 at Skopje, Macedonia. There is some confusion about her date of birth, some say it is August 27, while others, quoting Mother Teresa herself, say that she was actually born the previous day, August 26, and christened (given a name in Church) on August 27. Her parents named her Agnes Gonxha Bojaxhiu, pronounced AG-nes GOHN-ja BOY-yah-jee-oo. That's rather a big name for someone who remained so tiny, even as a grown up, isn't it?'

'Agnes Gonxha was the youngest child of her parents, Nikolle and Dranafile Bojaxhiu. They had five children in all, but only three survived–Aga, a girl, Lazer, their only son, and of course Agnes.'

'Nikolle and Drana originally belonged to Prizren in the south of Kosovo, Albania, and were Roman Catholics. Many Albanians are Muslims, and the majority of Macedonian Christians belong to the Orthodox Church, which is different from the Catholic Church, but Agnes' family was devoutly Catholic. This had a big influence on her life, obviously.'

'They lived next door to the Sacred Heart Church in Skopje, and Agnes probably helped her mother and others arrange the flowers in church and decorate it during festivals. She has also told some of the people who interviewed her that she sang in the church choir and was also a member of the church's youth group.'

'Yes, but was there anything different about her as a child?' asked Neetu.

'There are no reports of the child Agnes being unusually or extraordinary interested in the church', said Mrs Patel. 'She was just a member of a family which considered its religion very important.'

'Agnes' brother Laser has talked about how the family was quite well-to-do. Nikolle was a successful contractor and was able to provide many comforts for his wife and children. Theirs was a happy, loving family.'

'But Nikolle was also involved in politics. Skopje in the early 1900s had a mixed population of people from different religious and cultural backgrounds, very much like India. It was also a centre for rebellion against the Ottoman Empire, and Nikolle Bojaxhiu was involved in the rebellion.'

'When Agnes was about eight years old, Nikolle died suddenly. Some say that he died of a heart attack, others say his death was the result of his involvement in politics. But whatever the cause, Agnes must have missed her father dreadfully.'

'Drana was now left with the task of providing for her family single handed, as Aga was only about 14 and Lazer was just one year older than Agnes.'

'Younger than us', said Neena.

'Luckily, Drana was talented in sewing, and took in work, making clothes and doing embroidery', continued their mother. 'With this she was able to see to her children's needs and the family continued to be loving and united.'

'But life must have been hard', said Neetu, looking thoughtful.'

Mrs Patel nodded, and continued her story.

'Agnes was a normal girl, and had an ordinary girl's dream of getting married and living an ordinary life. But when she was around 15 years old, the family went on a little trip to the mountains. On the way up, they stopped several times to pray at religious statuettes along the road. At one such stop, Agnes said later, she heard a voice telling her to 'follow God and serve.' She did not make any on-the-spot commitment or decision. But it must surely have remained in her mind.'

'The experience on the mountain road must have combined with her interest in stories of the terrible suffering of the poor in the world that she had heard in classrooms, and about the good work being done by nuns to help the poor. Gradually, ideas must have started coming to her, slowly she must have come to realise what she really wanted to do. She wanted to become a nun and serve the poor.'

'As she later told one of her biographers – that's the name for people who write the story of the lives of famous people – the only problem was her loving family. Agnes was very happy at home, and like any other young girl, found the thought of leaving her mother, sister and brother and going far away very hard.'

'Oh Mamma, I would hate to leave you and Papa and Neena and go away by myself', said Neetu.

'But it was a decision that Agnes had to take', said Mrs Patel.

'Agnes had a particular interest in helping girls. The sisters of Loreto, an order of nuns based in Ireland, were educators and missionaries and had a mission in

Bengal here in India, to teach girls. She applied to the Catholic Church for permission to join the Loreto Sisters.'

'When she was 18, permission came from the Church in Rome for her to travel to Dublin, to the Convent of the Loreto Sisters, and work towards becoming a nun.'

'When it came to the point, it must have been very difficult for the young girl to leave her beloved home and take the long voyage to Ireland, which would be only the first step of an even longer journey, to know that she would have to learn new languages and live and work in unfamiliar places among unfamiliar people.'

'But Agnes bravely left Skopje for Ireland. She would never see her mother again. Drana lost her youngest daughter, but hundreds of people gained a 'mother.'

Mrs Patel saw that the twins were both looking a little sad. 'Why don't you go out and play for a little while?' she suggested. We can continue the story after dinner.'

3

'Yesterday is gone. Tomorrow has not yet come. We have only today. Let us begin.'

'Have you finished your homework children?' asked Mrs. Patel.

'Yes, Mamma', replied Neetu. 'We've tidied our room and set out our uniforms for tomorrow', added Neena. 'Will you continue Mother Teresa's story?'

'OK, so where was I?' asked Mrs Patel, settling down on the sofa, with the two girls on either side of her.

'You were telling us how Agnes left home when she was 18 to go to Ireland, which was far away and completely unknown to her', said Neetu.

'Right', said her mother. 'Agnes Gonxha went to a place called Rathfarnham near Dublin, to the Sisters of Loreto. There she was given basic instruction in the life and duties of a nun. She also learned English. Another girl who was also a novice, as young women who are starting to learn how to become nuns are called, later remembered Agnes as a quiet, shy and small girl.'

'She spent a very short time at Rathfarnham, around six to eight weeks. In January of 1929, Agnes Gonxha started her journey by ship to Calcutta. The Loreto Sisters had started schools in India to educate young women, and Agnes was eager to join the effort.'

'But before that, she had to continue her education as a nun. You know, children, the process is known as novitiate in the Catholic Church. For this, she was sent to Darjeeling, a hill station in the foothills of the Himalayas. There, Agnes was trained in the life she would be required to live as a woman dedicated to the service of Christ. She also had to learn the local languages – Bengali and Hindi – besides English, as she would need these to live in Calcutta and teach there.'

'Oh goodness, I can't even manage Hindi as a second language', murmured Neetu. 'Imagine having to learn so many new languages.'

'Yes, it must have been hard', agreed her mother, smiling. 'But, as you will see, Agnes was a very determined young lady.

'At Darjeeling, Agnes took her first vows as a nun in 1931. The novitiate is a fairly long process, as both the person who wishes to be a nun as well as her superiors in the Church have to be sure that she is suited for the discipline and hardships that she will need to undertake throughout her life later. It is something like your school education system, and you pass it in stages. As the young women go through the process and make commitments to serve Christ and the church, they are asked to change the name their parents gave them, and taken on another name.'

'Oh NO!', said Neena, horrified. 'I wouldn't like to be called anything other than Neena. Would you, Neetu?'

As her twin shook her head, their mother said 'This practice is followed in other religions too, children. It stands for renouncing or giving up your former self and becoming a *new person*.'

'The novices usually choose the name of some Saint or religious figure who means a lot to them personally, and whose example they wish to follow. Agnes Gonxha chose the name of Teresa for herself, to honour Teresa of Avila and Thérèse de Lisieux, both Saints of the Catholic Church. Thérèse de Lisieux was specially dear to her as the patron Saint of foreign Missionaries, and known as the *Little Flower of Jesus.*'

'She continued in the novitiate, and in 1937 Sister Teresa took her final vows and became a full-fledged nun.'

'Even as a novice nun, Sister Teresa was given a teaching job. She taught first in a school in Darjeeling, and then was posted at St.Mary's High School, Calcutta. This was a school for girls from middle-class and well-to-do Indian and Anglo-Indian families.'

'Sister Teresa loved teaching. Her subjects were History, Geography and Catechism (teaching the principles of the catholic faith).'

'Yes, we know, Mama', said Neetu. 'When we have Moral Science class, the Christian children in our school go to catechism class.'

'Right. Anyway, to get back to Mother Teresa, the school where she taught was lovely, with well-kept gardens and nice classrooms, the students were bright young girls, very like the students in your school now', said Mrs Patel.

'Life must have seemed very good to the young nun. She really enjoyed her vocation – that's a word for an occupation which is something more than just a job, something you have a passion to do. A nun or a priest or anyone who dedicates himself or herself to the service of God or a cause must have a special call to do so, and it is described as a "vocation". Agnes Gonxha had answered such a call to become Sister Teresa, and life with the Loreto nuns suited her very well.'

'People who have written about her or made movies about her have tried to find out what she was like as one of the Loreto nuns. They found that she wasn't remembered for anything special. In Rathfarnham someone had described her as 'ordinary', and that was the impression in Calcutta too. She was well-liked as a teacher, but did not distinguish herself in any other way. She spent about twenty years teaching, and quietly moved up the scale until she became Principal of St.Mary's High School.'

'Talking of this part of her life, Mother Teresa was to say later, "At Loreto, I was the happiest nun in the world". But the happiness and contentment did not last very long.'

'The Calcutta of those days was a city of huge contrasts. It was a city of very cultured, intelligent people. It was the home of many rich families. Calcutta was initially the capital or the headquarters of the British in India, and at one level, its society was very polished and sophisticated, with access to a lot of luxuries.'

'At another level, Calcutta was noted for extremely unhygienic conditions, the city was home to a massive number of poor and destitute people who lived in unimaginable dirt and squalor, with no facilities for food, leave alone shelter and healthcare.'

'Sister Teresa in her room at the Convent could see both these faces of Calcutta. She lived in clean and well-ordered surroundings and interacted with refined young women within the campus. But when she looked out of her bedroom window, she could see the slums beyond the compound walls. She saw the terrible living conditions of people there, the extreme poverty, the sickness and death. When she went out of the convent, she saw sick and old people dying on the roads, alone and uncared for. The contrast must surely have disturbed her.'

'In the September of 1946, Sister Teresa went again to the mountains, to Darjeeling. For one, she was ill, she was suspected to have contracted tuberculosis. She needed rest and fresh air to recover. Also, it was time for a spiritual retreat – a time of quiet reflection that Catholics undertake regularly, a time spent away from the stress and strain of routine life, a time to catch up with spiritual matters without disturbance.'

'Sister Teresa went to Darjeeling by train. It must have been a very beautiful journey, as it still is, up the slopes of the lower Himalayas. On that journey, just like on the other mountain journey in her native Macedonia when she was 15, Sister Teresa received another call – 'a call within a call', as she described it. While praying, she heard a quiet voice telling her to leave everything and follow Christ into the slums. In Sister Teresa's own words: "The message was quite clear: I was to leave the convent and help the poor whilst living among them. It was an order."

'She called this "Inspiration Day". That day changed her life completely, and brought about total change in the life of countless others as well.'

'Now, that's enough for now. It's bedtime. We'll continue tomorrow', said Mrs. Patel, and the twins went yawning to bed.

4

'We can do no great things, only small things with great love'

The next evening, Mrs Patel continued the story of Mother Teresa over tea.

'Yesterday I told you how Sister Teresa received a "call within a call". Today I'll tell you how she answered this second call', said Mrs Patel.

'The convent, the place where nuns live, away from the daily life of the world, has very strict rules about going out, having visitors and even the type of work to be done. After her trip to Darjeeling, Sister Teresa began to try and get permission to live and work outside the convent.'

'This is no easy task even today. All those years ago it must have been very difficult to even raise the subject. You see, when a nun enters a particular order, she agrees to live by the rules that govern that order for the rest of her life, and obey the instructions of her superiors without question. To convince people in authority to give permission to even change the rules slightly is long and tedious. So you can imagine how hard it must have been for her to get permission to come out of the order itself and work according to her own rules and be responsible for herself.'

'But Sister Teresa was sure that she had received a specific command from Christ, and that she needed to follow it. 'I knew where I belonged but I did not know how to get there', she said later, talking about this point in her life.'

'She must have faced many hurdles along the way. But she displayed a side of her nature that probably not many had seen before. It was a trait that she would demonstrate several more times. She was very persistent in working to achieve what she wanted, and believed to be right.'

'It took four long years, but finally, in 1948, permission came from the Pope in Rome, the supreme head of the

Roman Catholic Church throughout the world, for her to be uncloistered.'

'What's that Mamma" asked Neena.

'Cloistered is a word meaning secluded or isolated', explained her mother. 'In the convent, nuns are kept separate from regular life in the outside world. They have their own routines of prayer and service. Uncloistered is the opposite of that.'

'But this did not mean that Sister Teresa was giving up or going back on the vows she had taken when she became a nun. She would continue to be dedicated to the service of Christ. It only meant that she was allowed to leave the convent and go out into the world.'

'That year, she also took Indian citizenship. So she got another new identity.'

'At last Sister Teresa was free to be with the poorest of the poor, as she had been told to do.'

'But she now found herself alone. She no longer had the shelter or the protection of the convent, the support of the family atmosphere there, with the nuns sharing their work, their meals and their worship.'

'I looked up some books about Mother Teresa, and I found that this is what she herself had to say about this time', said Mrs Patel, taking out a piece of paper and reading from it:

'I left the Loreto Sisters in 1948. Leaving was my greatest sacrifice, and the most difficult thing I have ever done. It was much more difficult than to leave my family and country to enter religious life. But I had the inner command to renounce Loreto to go to serve the poor in the streets, and I had the blessing of obedience.'

'She must surely have been nervous and even little scared to find herself so suddenly back in the everyday world', Mrs Patel continued. 'She would have had to cope with so many things she must have forgotten about, looking for a house, getting provisions, meeting people of various kinds, having to ask for help. But her faith must have kept her safe. She took comfort from a verse in the Bible which says *God will provide*.'

'Sister Teresa realized that if she wanted to help the sick and the dying among the poor, she would need some special training. So she went to Patna where she took a short course in nursing. Then she returned to Calcutta, and found temporary accommodation with the Little Sisters of the Poor, another group of nuns.'

'Almost immediately, she came across a poor woman dying on the street. There was nothing much the nun could do to help ease her physical pain. But she stayed with her and made her as comfortable as possible. When the woman died, she died knowing that she was no longer alone, there was someone who cared with her. Sister Teresa knew then that she was on the right track – this was what she had been called to do.'

She later said: "After leaving Loreto, I was on the street, with no shelter, no company, no helper, no money, no employment, no promise, no guarantee, no security. I prayed, God, You, only You. I trust in Your call, Your inspiration. You will not let me down. I needed a roof to shelter the abandoned, so I started to search."

'Well, God answered her prayer. She found a room of her own, just a tiny place in the slum, very different from her room at the convent, which, though it wouldn't have had any luxurious things, must have been clean and warm at least.'

'She decided to give up wearing the uniform of the nuns, called a habit, which was basically Western. Instead, she chose to wear the Indian saree, but not just any saree. She decided to always use a simple white cotton saree with a blue-striped border, which she wore draped over her head. On her left shoulder she pinned a silver crucifix. That's an image of Christ on the cross.'

'But were the people friendly to her Mamma?' asked Neena.

'No, not at first', admitted Mrs Patel.

'Sister Teresa decided that she would start by doing what she had been trained to do all these years – teach. She had no classroom, leave alone a school. She had no blackboard, duster or chalk piece. But she did not let that get her down.'

'She settled herself down under a tree in the slum, and invited the poor children to gather around her. They had had no chance to get even the most basic education. Sister Teresa picked up a stout twig and started teaching the children – not English but the alphabets of Bengali, their own native language. She also tried to teach them basic hygiene.'

'Gradually, this little woman won the trust of the slum dwellers. And, more surprisingly, she found that she wasn't alone. One by one people started joining her. She must have been astonished when she saw some of those who came to lend her a hand – they were her own former students, girls from well-respected, wealthy, cultured families who would probably have wrinkled up their noses at the smell if they were forced to pass the slums earlier. These young women exchanged their costly sarees for the white-and-blue ones that Sister Teresa wore, and worked happily beside her.'

'Oh Mamma, that must have made Sister Teresa really happy', said Neetu, her eyes shining.

'Yes', agreed her mother. 'She not only had volunteers, she also had donations coming in, gifts in the form of money, medicines and other necessities.'

'But she also had problems. She was abused by the very people she was trying to help. She was accused by many of trying to convert the slum dwellers to Christianity under the pretext of helping them, she was even stoned. Again, that persistent part of her character was displayed. Sister Teresa did not give up or let the problems force her to shift from the path she had chosen. She just kept on doing what she felt she was meant to do.'

'She was now leading a group of 12, and the Holy Roman Church approved of the group being called Missionaries of Charity. At first the group was under the control of the Archdiocese of Calcutta, which meant that their immediate superior was the Bishop of Calcutta. But later, Rome took direct control of the order.'

'The nuns who joined Mother Teresa, as she was now called, had to take the usual three vows – of poverty, chastity and obedience, but they had to take a fourth one as well – they had to promise to serve the poor throughout their lives.'

'Mother Teresa was very particular that her nuns lived just like the poorest of the poor. They were to own nothing but one change of clothes and some very essential items, including a bucket and a scrubbing brush!'

'And so began a mission to care for the very poorest, and make sure that no man, woman or child suffered from the greatest poverty of all, the sense of being unloved and unwanted.'

'After dinner, I'll tell you how the movement grew and grew and grew….'

5

'The most terrible poverty is loneliness and the feeling of being unloved.'

After dinner, Mrs Patel took up the tale again.

'So, children, we have seen how Mother Teresa started her work among the poorest of the poor as a teacher. Her open-air classes slowly picked up, and she taught the children of the slums not only the Bengali letters but also basic cleanliness.

'While she was passing on knowledge to this neglected section of society, she was also concerned with another group which was even more neglected – in fact, this group was totally ignored, she found. When people grew too old to look after themselves, when some bad disease struck them down, they were simply abandoned. They were just left to lie around, without shelter or food, in the filthiest of conditions, till at last they died and the intolerable suffering ended.

'Mother Teresa made it her mission to care for these sick and dying people, whose suffering was so greatly increased because they knew that they were unwanted. She wanted these people to know that there was someone who cared, so that they might pass their last few days on this earth with dignity and die in peace.

'As the slum dwellers came to trust her, she gradually began visiting the sick and the dying in their homes and doing what she could to ease suffering. Slowly, people began turning to her for help, and appreciating the work she was doing. The more privileged people in Calcutta noticed what she was doing, and help began to come, as I told you earlier – in little drops first, and then, more generously. It came as donations of food, clothing, medicines, money and most important, volunteers.

'But she met with opposition too, remember.

'Yet, Mother Teresa quietly continued what she was doing. She and her group of sisters rented a room where they could care for the abandoned people. Obviously, it wasn't large enough.

'Then, in 1952, the Calcutta officials let her have an old hostel near an abandoned temple to the Goddess Kali. The area was called Kalighat, and Mother Teresa turned the place into her first free hospice for the poor. The Kalighat *Nirmal Hriday* was a place where the dying would be cared for.'

'*Nirmal* means pure, doesn't it Mamma?' asked Neetu.

'Yes, and *Hriday* means heart', added Neena.

'That's right, children', said their mother.

'One of the first people she took in was a former priest of the Kali temple who had been abandoned because he had got leprosy. Do you know what leprosy is?'

'I know it's some terrible skin disease', said Neena.

'It is a highly contagious disease – this means that it is quickly passed on from person to person', explained Mrs. Patel. 'These days it can be treated, but from very early days it was one of the most feared diseases. Even today you can see some lepers begging, with bleeding sores and bandages on their hands and feet, some in wheelchairs because they can't walk.'

'Neena, we see a beggar like that every day', said Neetu. 'Remember, at the traffic signal on the way to school?'

As her twin nodded, their mother said 'The government runs many institutions where such people can be cared for, but in those days there was no such facility, and those who were unfortunate enough to get leprosy were thrown out of their families and left to die. No one wanted to touch them or even come near them. Often, they were driven out of towns and villages into surrounding forests and uninhabited areas.'

'The Calcutta of those days had many lepers, begging or just dying on the streets, their sores covered by filthy rags and their arms and legs reduced to stumps. Kind hearted persons might drop a coin or two into their bowls, but that was the most these unfortunate people could expect.'

'So Mother Teresa's action of taking in the Hindu priest who was a leprosy patient and caring for him was a startling thing for the people of the area. This action of hers started a change in the attitude of those who had been criticising her. At *Nirmal Hriday*, the people saw the sisters washing and feeding and caring for destitute people whom no one wanted, and no other institution would accept. Slowly, opposition to her work started declining.'

'Then came the *Nirmal Hriday Shishu Bhavan*, an Orphanage, and in 1957, *Shanti Nagar*. The name means Peace Town. It was set up on land given by the Government. This was a village where leprosy patients and their families could live and move about freely and also carry on some occupation which would earn them some money. These were to remain the three main focus areas of the Missionaries of Charity – dying destitute people, lepers and orphaned or abandoned children. Caste and religion were not an issue. Anyone who was unloved and unwanted found acceptance with the sisters.'

'In 1959, the sisters started working outside Calcutta, and by the end of the 1960s, the Missionaries of Charity had set up homes and orphanages all over India.'

'In 1965, the Pope agreed to Mother Teresa's request to let her set up institutions outside India. The first home started by the Missionaries of Charity abroad was in Venezuela, and this was soon followed by others in various countries of Asia, Africa and Europe. The first centre in the United States was set up in the South Bronx area of New York.'

'In 1991, Mother Teresa returned home to Albania for the first time after leaving it when she was just 18 years old. She went there to open a Missionaries of Charity home in a place named *Tirana*.'

'As her work grew and flourished, more and more women began joining Mother Teresa's order. They moved to a three-storied building in Calcutta, which is even today known as Mother House. And still the order grew.'

'Was it only women who joined the Missionaries of Charity?' asked Neetu.

'Good question', said Mrs Patel. 'Mother Teresa found that men were also needed, to care for boys in orphanages and for men in the hospices. There were also some places that were too dangerous for her sisters. So she started the Missionary Brothers of Charity.'

'The Missionaries of Charity started one of the first hospices to care for AIDS patients – in California, USA, in1987. The sisters also care for refugees, the aged, the disabled, alcoholics and victims of natural disaster and famines.'

'Mother Teresa personally visited victims of disasters in Ethiopia, Chernobyl, Armenia and even the war torn areas of Palestine.'

'When Mother Teresa passed away in 1997, the Missionaries of Charity was operating 610 centres in 123 countries.'

'Though donations and recognition flooded in, Mother Teresa always insisted that the sisters and brothers in her order live their lives exactly as the poorest of the poor do, and dedicate themselves to serving the destitute and the unwanted. She was sure that they would find joy in doing this. Life was extremely hard, but, as she said: 'Poverty for us is a freedom… It is a joyful freedom. There is no television here, no this, no that; but we are perfectly happy.'

'Now, isn't that a wonderful thing? Do you think you girls would be happy if you had no TV, no stereo players, no CDs?'

'Hmm… no TV, no CDs…, that'll be tough', said the twins, as their mother smiled. 'OK, bedtime', she said, shooing her daughters into their room. 'We'll continue after school tomorrow.'

The twins wished her Goodnight and got ready for bed. Both were thinking of life without all the comforts they had got used to, and were wondering if they would be really happy without them.

6

'I am God's pencil'

Mrs Patel took up the story the next evening at teatime, while Neena and Neetu listened attentively.

'Yesterday I told you how Mother Teresa started her work alone, and how the order grew beyond everyone's imagination. We saw how it spread outside Calcutta to other parts of India, and to so many other countries in all the continents.'

'What an extraordinary achievement, wasn't it girls.'

'She must have been an extraordinary person to have done all that. What made Mother Teresa extraordinary Mamma?' asked Neetu.

'That's difficult to say', replied her mother. 'But I've been reading up about her life. I'll talk about some incidents from her life, which have been narrated either by Mother Teresa herself or by those who knew her. They might give us some idea of what made her different from others.'

'We know that Mother Teresa was physically a small, frail woman. We have all seen pictures of her as an old lady, her face covered in wrinkles. But we've also noticed her wide, happy smile in those pictures, and her sparkling eyes. She was also very brisk and active. She had the habit of walking very fast. "It is impossible to walk fast and be unhappy," she had once said.'

'Happiness was one of the extraordinary traits of her character. You would think that a person who is looking at suffering and misery all day long, year after year, would be miserable herself. But not Mother Teresa and her sisters. To repeat her own words, which I told you about yesterday, she said: "We are perfectly happy". When you're happy doing what you're doing, you find yourself doing better than your best, isn't it?'

The two girls nodded thoughtfully.

'Another trait was her persistence', continued Mrs Patel. 'She refused to let go. I'm sure you can think of at least a couple of occasions when you've wanted something badly, and Papa and I weren't very enthusiastic about letting you have it, but we finally agreed to your request because you kept asking for it and trying to convince us that you needed that thing. Mother Teresa was a little like that.'

'Remember when she first wanted to come out of the Loreto order and start working on her own? When she applied for permission, no one was ready to say "yes, OK, go ahead". But she kept trying. When the Bishop of Calcutta was reluctant to let her have her way, she kept on writing to him. She described herself as 'a little nothing', but kept on saying that she had got a call to 'take Jesus into the slums' and serve the poorest of the poor. She suggested that if he was unable to decide, he should ask higher authorities. She refused to take 'No' for an answer, until finally, permission came from the Pope himself.'

'David Aikman, a well-known journalist, who wrote about Mother Teresa, tells of an incident when Mother came across a dying woman who was being nibbled at by rats. Imagine how horrible that must have been. She asked a nearby hospital to take the poor lady in, but the staff there was reluctant to do so. Mother Teresa simply refused to move from the spot till they agreed to her request. Remember Gandhiji and the '*sathyagraha*' movement which won India freedom? That was a similar technique, wasn't it?'

'Also, she was not afraid to speak her mind, even to Presidents and Prime Ministers. She held some strong opinions on controversial issues like divorce and killing unborn children, and expressed them boldly even though she knew that powerful people may not like it. She spoke bravely on these subjects on several occasions to the Indian government and even to the then President of the USA, Bill Clinton.'

'What made Mother Teresa so brave?' asked Neena.

'Good question!' said Mrs. Patel. 'I believe it was something called "moral authority". She believed that she had the authority to say these things because she knew she had been doing her duty sincerely and was totally obedient to God's instructions.'

'This confidence that she was doing God's will made Mother Teresa, who was by nature shy and mild, bold and willing to take chances.'

'One of her biographers talks about an incident during the early years of her service to the poor in Calcutta. She went to a busy pharmacy and waited meekly while crowds of customers were served. When a pharmacist was free she stepped forward with a long list, and asked him whether he would like to "do something beautiful for God". I'm sure that without the confidence of moral authority she would never have thought of taking such a step. But her confidence wasn't misplaced. She walked out of the pharmacy that day with a whole load of supplies donated by the pharmacy.'

'Have you noticed Mother Teresa's hands, children?' asked Mrs Patel.

'No, not really', said Neetu.

Why, whats special about them?', asked her twin.

'She constantly held a rosary – a special string of beads used by Catholics which help them in their prayers. The rosary has a special connection to Virgin Mary, the mother of Jesus, who is particularly beloved to Catholics. Mother Teresa once said that by holding the rosary she felt she was holding hands with Mother Mary. Holding the rosary, her wrinkled and twisted hands soothed suffering people and brought them peace.'

'The Bible talks of three great qualities in a good human being – Faith, Hope and Love – and says the greatest of these is love. Love was perhaps the greatest of

Mother Teresa's qualities. She had so much love in her. 'We have been created to love and be loved', she said. It was this love that helped her to ignore her own comforts and needs, and give herself completely to the poor.'

'Sister Nirmala, who succeeded her as head of the Missionaries of Charity, during an interview with a magazine, remembered an incident when she was a new entrant in the order. She was a 'nobody', at that time. She fell sick and Mother Teresa took her from the section where she was living with other new entrants, and brought her to her own room. There was no extra bed in the room, and Mother Teresa put the young nun into her own bed, and slept on the table herself. 'I was very new in the order. I was just a small little one, you know, and she was Mother – big Mother', Sister Nirmala told the interviewer. 'Do you understand the meaning of that? These little things of love were common with Mother: her delicate love.'

'So we get the picture of a little old lady who was extremely confident that she was doing God's will, and so had the right to say and do things that would let her continue to do His will. This confidence gave the courage to speak her mind boldly, and to persist till she got what she wanted, even if people were not initially willing to let her have her way. She was also an amazingly happy person who was filled with extraordinary love, which helped her to put everyone else before herself.'

'I think Mother Teresa doesn't sound very real, Mamma?' commented Neetu.

'Doesn't she?' smiled her mother. 'But I promise you she was real. She had several little qualities which proved that she was just as human as you or me.'

'For one, she was capable of getting angry. Something that really annoyed her was waste. She had seen extreme poverty in the slums of India and in places like Ethiopia, where hundreds of people were dying because of the lack of even the most basic of needs, food, shelter and clothing. She would compare this situation to the thoughtless waste of resources in rich countries, and she would get angry. In her own words: "When I see waste here (the USA) I feel angry on the inside. I don't approve of myself being angry but it's something you can't help after seeing Ethiopia."'

'One of the sisters in her order once told an interviewer about how Mother liked to "settle things". Haven't you seen your aunts and me busily going about the house putting things back in their proper places?

Well, Mother Teresa was something like that. She was always going about tidying things and keeping them away.'

'And guess what? She loved to eat sweets!'

The twins laughed. 'Oh, that truly makes her sound like a real person', said Neena.

'Yes', agreed Mrs Patel. 'Mother Teresa was an ordinary person who, because she let herself be totally obedient to God's call, was able to achieve extraordinary things. She never thought of herself as great or blessed with amazing qualities. She knew her own weaknesses, but trusted that God would provide what was necessary for His work to be carried out.'

'Once, talking of the 'Voice' which called her to leave the convent and go out in the slums, she said Jesus had told her: 'You are I know the most incapable person – weak and sinful but just because you are that – I want to use You for My glory. Will you refuse?'

'She did not refuse.'

7

'God doesn't require us to succeed; he only requires that you try.'

'Mamma', said Neena while the family was having dinner that night, 'you were telling us this evening that Mother Teresa was a person who did extraordinary things. But when did people start realising that she was doing all these extraordinary things? When did she become famous?'

'What's all this about Mother Teresa?' asked Mr Patel. He had been away from home for the last few days and didn't know why his wife and the twins were talking about her. So all of them took turns to tell him about the planned visit to the orphanage, and how the subject of Mother Teresa had come up.

'So Mamma is telling us what she knows and what she's read up about Mother Teresa', explained Neetu.

'Well, I can tell you how a lot of people outside India and not connected with the Catholic Church first came to hear of Mother Teresa', said Mr Patel. 'It was because of a documentary film made by a British Journalist named Malcolm Muggeridge. It was called *Something Beautiful for God*, and Muggeridge filmed Mother Teresa and her Missionaries of Charity going about their work among the poor, the sick and the dying.

'It was a very, very effective film, and it was screened at very many places all over the world. People were shocked at the terrible conditions that the poor people were living in, and they were very impressed by the wonderful work being done by the Missionaries of Charity.'

'Muggeridge himself started out on the assignment as a sceptic, someone who doesn't really believe in God, but somewhere along the way, he became convinced of the absolute sincerity with which Mother Teresa worked, and he himself became a devout Catholic.'

'Did Mother Teresa convert people to Christianity?' asked Neena.

'That was something which people who were opposed to her often accused her of doing', replied her father. 'But Mother Teresa herself had a different definition for conversion than the one we know. We use the word to mean somehow persuading people to change the religion into which they were born, and accept another faith. But Mother Teresa used to say that if, by our actions, we convinced someone to come closer to God, that was *conversion*.'

'In fact, children, I remember a passage from a book by a man named Desmond Doig. He was quoting Mother Teresa's views on conversion. She told him 'What we are all trying to do by our work, by serving the people, is to come closer to God. If in coming face to face with God we accept Him in our lives, then we are *converting*. We become a better Hindu, a better Muslim, a better Catholic, a better whatever we are, and then by being better we come closer and closer to Him... What approach would I use? For me, naturally, it would be a Catholic one, for you it may be Hindu, for someone else, Buddhist, according to one's conscience. What God is in your mind you must accept.'

'On other occasions, she said "There is only one God and He is God to all; therefore it is important that everyone is seen as equal before God. I've always said we should help a Hindu become a better Hindu, a Muslim become a better Muslim, a Catholic become a better Catholic. We believe our work should be our example to people... There are so many religions and each one has its different ways of following God. I follow Christ."'

'Does that answer your question, Neena?'

'Yes, Papa', said Neena. 'But just now you said that people opposed to her accused her of trying to convert people to Christianity. Why were people opposed to her when she was doing so much good?'

'Well, Neena', said Mr. Patel, 'there will always be people who oppose those who are public figures.'

'What's a public figure Papa?' asked Neetu.

'Someone who's become well-known', answered her father. 'When Mother Teresa and her work became known to people all over the world, there were some who criticised her for various things.'

'Some people were not satisfied with the way money was managed by the Missionaries of Charity. There were others who were unhappy with the way the hospices were run. This was a major criticism. Many people felt that Mother Teresa and her sisters were not focussing enough on making the sick better. They didn't have enough qualified doctors and nurses to treat patients and cure them. They were concentrating on giving loving care, instead of working to heal illnesses. They felt this was the wrong focus.'

'Mother Teresa understood that in this world, you will need to face criticism and opposition. She didn't let such comments worry her too much. When people asked her what she had to say to her critics, she replied: 'No matter who says what, you should accept it with a smile and do your own work.'

One filmmaker who was making a documentary about her asked her what she felt when people called her names like *Hell's Angel* and *Ghoul of Calcutta.* She replied with a smile: 'God takes away your good name, you accept it. If you're on the street, you accept being in the street. Sometimes that's how it is – everything is taken away from you.'

Mrs. Patel saw that both the twins were looking very sad. Neetu had tears in her eyes.

'You know, children', she said, 'while Mother Teresa had several critics, there were thousands and thousands of others who admired her. She was given many gifts and won many prestigious prizes and awards, both in India and abroad.'

'Do you know how she got money to set up *Shanti Nagar*, her first colony for lepers? The Pope, who is the head of the Catholic Churches in the world, had come on a visit to India, and he was gifted a very expensive car. He in turn gifted it to Mother Teresa. She used it as the prize for a raffle, and with the money collected from selling the raffle tickets, set up the colony.'

'India gave her the Padma Shri award for distinguished service in 1962 and the Nehru Prize for promotion of international peace and understanding ten years later.'

'From USA, she got the Presidential Medal of Freedom, that country's highest civilian award, in 1985. She was also given an honorary US Citizenship in 1996, becoming only the fifth person to be given such an honour.'

'She was chosen for the Pope John XXIII Peace Prize in1971 and received the Balzan Prize in 1979. She also got the Templeton and Magsaysay awards. In 1975 she was conferred the Albert Schweitzer International Prize.'

'Mother Teresa accepted all awards on behalf of the poor, and used money that came with the prizes to fund her work.'

'She was given honorary degrees from Harvard and Cambridge Universities and addressed the United Nations on its 40th anniversary in 1985, which was a huge honour.'

'But perhaps the greatest honour was the Nobel Prize. She was chosen for this in 1979. The committee which selected her for the award said: "She contributed to international peace by bridging the gulf that exists between the rich nations and the poor nations." A famous US newspaper commented that in choosing Mother Teresa for the award, the world was reminded that there is more than one kind of peace and that politics is not the only way to find it.'

'Mother Teresa accepted the award, and went to Oslo, the capital of Norway, to receive it. Now, Norway is an extremely cold country. Mother Teresa went wearing just her usual thin saree and white sandals. Those who are given awards generally make a speech while receiving it. In her speech, Mother Teresa said 'Personally I am unworthy. I accept in the name of the poor because I believe that by giving me the prize they have recognized the presence of the poor of the world.'

'When someone asked her 'What can we do to promote world peace?' she answered: 'Go home and love your family.'

'She used the award money to fund her work. She also said she did not want the traditional banquet to honour her as a recipient of the world's highest award. The cost of the banquet would have been $6,000. For the first time in history the banquet was cancelled and instead, the money was given to her. She used it to provide 15,000 meals to the poor.'

'Wow! She was one great lady', said Neetu. 'But how did she die? Is the Missionaries of Charity still doing well?'

'I'll tell you about that tomorrow, girls', said Mrs Patel. It's past your bedtime, so clear up and go straight to bed.'

The twins groaned as they got up to obey their mother. They would have to wait till tea-time the next day for the story to continue.

8

'I have all eternity to rest, and there is still much to do'

'Well, children', said Mrs Patel, 'we're nearing the end of our story.'

'We've talked about Mother Teresa's early life, about how she decided to become a nun and serve the people in poor countries, how she was determined to form her own order, how she persisted and won permission to do that, how her Missionaries of Charity grew from a one woman show to an organization having thousands of people, men and women, under its fold. We discussed the personality of this remarkable woman and the praise as well as the criticism that she received.

'She started her life as a nun when she was 18 years old, just a few years older than you girls are now', said Mrs Patel, watching her daughters enjoy the crisp samosas she'd made for their tea.

'Since then, she lived a demanding life, physically as well as emotionally. She had so many things to see to, so many decisions to take. She was always busy.'

'Obviously, all this had an effect on her health. After about 40 years of hectic life, she started having heart trouble. In 1989, she suffered a heart attack. A pacemaker was implanted in her body.'

'What's that Mamma?' asked Neetu.

'That's a mechanical device to help people with weak hearts', explained her mother. 'Those who need it have to undergo a surgery to put it in.'

'Mother Teresa was asked to take things easy, and she wanted to resign her position as head of the Missionaries of Charity, but no one suitable was found to take over from her. So she continued with her work, just as before. She even went abroad, on what must have been very difficult, long trips, to visit her institutions in various countries.'

'But, though her spirit appeared to be fit and fine, her body couldn't keep up. By March 1997, she was too weak to carry out the many responsibilities that rested on her as head of the Missionaries of Charity. This time, there was someone who could take much of the burden from her shoulders. Sister Nirmala, who I spoke to you about the other day, was elected to succeed her as Superior General of the order.'

'On September 5th of that year, Mother Teresa finished her dinner and prayers at Motherhouse. She then began to find it difficult to breathe. Those who were closest to her came to be with her. She told them of her great love for Jesus. And finally, her heart just stopped beating. She was 87 years old.'

'All across the world, people, ranging from common men and women to very important public figures, mourned her death. The Dalai Lama, who is the spiritual leader of the Tibetans, paying tribute to her, said she was 'an example of the human capacity to generate infinite love, compassion and altruism.'

'Our own President and Prime Minister and many other national and international leaders expressed their grief at the passing away of such an extraordinary lady.'

'I think Jacques Chirac, who was the President of France at that time, said the most moving words.

Reacting to the news of Mother Teresa's death, he said "This evening, there is less love, less compassion, less light in the world."'

'If people in far away places were so upset, can you imagine the sorrow that people of Calcutta felt?'

'Her body was kept on public view at Motherhouse so that people could pay their homage to her. A great stream of VIPs came, of course, but there was an even greater crowd of the poor and underprivileged – beggars, the sick, the lame, the poor and the downtrodden. They felt they had suffered a huge loss.'

'The Indian government gave her a state funeral. That is an honour which is given only to very few people to recognize their valuable contribution to our country.'

'Mother Teresa was buried near the chapel at Motherhouse. Her tombstone has a verse from the Bible written on it – words that Jesus spoke to his disciples: *'Love one another as I have loved you.'*

The two girls were silent for some time, thinking about the life and work of the wonderful little nun from Albania.

'Is that the end of the story Mamma?' asked Neena.

'Well, no, that's not really the end', said Mrs Patel with a smile. 'There's a little bit more. But you'll have to wait till dinner to hear it, as you have your homework to do, and I have my cooking.'

9

'I am only trying to live my love. Let us do something beautiful for God.'

'So children', began Mrs Patel that night ... 'I told you how Mother Teresa worked as hard as she could, and was actively involved with the Missionaries of Charity right till the last day of her life. I told you how the world mourned when she passed away. Now, most stories would end with that... the death of the main character. But in the case of people like Mother Teresa, the stories really don't end. They go on.'

Neetu and Neena listened to their mother as they helped her lay the table for tea.

'Some important developments have taken place in Mother Teresa's life after she died', said Mrs Patel.

Both girls burst out laughing. 'How can things happen in a person's life after she's dead, Mamma?' asked Neetu.

'Yes, that sounds funny, doesn't it?' agreed Mrs Patel. 'But I don't know how else to put it. After she died, the Catholic Church has started a process for declaring her a saint.'

'What process, Mamma?' asked Neena. 'She was obviously such a good person, so of course she's a saint.'

'It's not as simple as that, Neena', said her mother. 'The Catholic Church follows a strict procedure which takes a lot of time before it acknowledges a man or woman as a Saint. There are so many conditions to be met, and it is done in stages.'

'First of all, the process can't begin till five years have passed since that person's death. But in some cases, the Pope can decide not to insist on this condition. He did that for Mother Teresa, and the procedure started in 1999, just two years after she passed away.'

'First, the Bishop of the area in which the person lived, and people who knew him or her well have to inform the Pope that this person is fit for sainthood. This is called *Cause of Saints.*'

'Once the Pope is convinced that the person is a fit candidate for sainthood, then he appoints a Postulator to talk to the people who were involved with the person. In Mother Teresa's case, the Postulator interviewed lots and lots of people and collected piles of information about her life and thoughts.'

'This material was gone through by someone called a Relater, who put it all together in a document called Position Paper. This gave the Pope a clear idea of what Mother Teresa was like.'

'The Position Paper on Mother Teresa showed the Pope that here was a person of 'heroic virtue', or exceptional goodness. And so the Pope gave her the title of '*venerable*' which means admired, respected or even revered.'

'The next step the Church takes is to give the title of 'Blessed' to a person. This is called Beatification. For this, the Church must have a record of at least one miracle that has happened to someone who has prayed to the dead person, asking that person to make a request to God. Usually, the miracles are something to do with health, because they are the ones which you can most easily find evidence about.'

'A number of people came forward to say how they had been cured through Mother Teresa's help. These included a Bengali lady who had stomach cancer and was healed and a Palestinian girl who was also cured of cancer after Mother Teresa appeared to her in a dream.'

'According to the Church's rules, the miracles must take place after the death of a person, because you can become a saint only after you're life has ended. But even during Mother Teresa's lifetime, at least one extraordinary event took place', said Mrs Patel. 'Do you remember Papa telling you about the film by Malcolm Muggeridge which made Mother Teresa famous?'

'Yes, Mamma', said Neena. 'It was called *Something Beautiful for God*', added Neetu.

'That's right, children', said Mrs Patel. 'Well, a lot of the shooting was done indoors. But the light was very poor, and Muggeridge said nothing would be seen in the film and was wondering how to get more lighting. Remember, in those days, photography wasn't as advanced as it is now. But Mother Teresa insisted that he just go ahead and shoot the film, without making any other arrangements.'

'So, just to make her happy, Muggeridge did the filming. And when they ran the film later, everyone was astonished to see that all the scenes shot indoors were filled with a beautiful, glowing light, and it was so very clear. They later used more of the same film to shoot some other indoor scenes not connected with Mother Teresa, and nothing could be seen!'

'Wow!' said the twins together.

'Well, Pope John Paul II, who was then the head of the Catholic Church, beatified Mother Teresa on October 19, 2003', continued Mrs Patel. She is known now as "Blessed Teresa of Calcutta". She also has a Feast Day. This is a day that is set apart by the church to honour a particular blessed person or saint. Mother Teresa's Feast Day is on September 5th.'

'Now the final step has to be taken – her canonisation, or conferring Sainthood on her. For this, the Pope has to approve more miracles that have happened because of praying to her for help.'

'The Missionaries of Charity and all those who admire Mother Teresa are waiting for this final step.'

'Meanwhile, the Missionaries of Charity continue Mother Teresa's work of serving the poorest of the poor, and as long as they do that, Mother Teresa's story will never end.'

The twins were silent after their mother finished speaking. Each of them was lost in their own thoughts about the extraordinary life of little Agnes from Albania who became Blessed Teresa of Calcutta.

'How did you like the story children?' asked Mrs Patel, breaking the silence.

'It was wonderful, Mama', said Neetu. 'Thank you for telling us about Mother Teresa', added Neena.

'We're going to visit the orphanage soon, Mamma', said Neetu. 'We need to think about what we're going to give the children.'

'Yes, we have to give until it hurts, like Mother Teresa said', put in Neena.

'You girls talk it over between yourselves and decide what you would like to give', said Mrs Patel. But don't think that you've done your bit just by going to the orphanage and giving something to the children. You must understand that there are poor people everywhere. And it's not only about food and shelter and money. Mother Teresa tried to teach the world that the greatest poverty was being unloved and unwanted. There may be such people even among your classmates. You must always see what you can do to help anyone in need.'

'Mamma, we'll try and do something beautiful for God', promised Neena.

'We'll try to do something every day', added Neetu.

And so, the story goes on…